FAMILY PLANET

poems by

Jim Scutti

Finishing Line Press
Georgetown, Kentucky

FINISHING LINE PRESS

www.finishinglinepress.com

FAMILY PLANET

ACKNOWLEDGMENTS

Many of the poems in Family Planet first appeared in the following
magazines:

Calliope: "I Remember Best," "Verotti Construction"
FutureCycle Poetry: "The Mystery Couple," Wood Stork"
Common Ground Review: "At the Abbotts Frozen Custard Stand," "Great
Blue Heron," "Route 19 West"
Comstock Review: "Family Planet"
Italian Americana: "Night Shift, Big Steel"
Slant: "At a Rest Stop on I-95 North," "On His Own Somewhere," "The
Greatest Spaghetti Maker in the World," "Smart"
The MainStreet Rag: "Things You Left," "MIA," "Perimeter Guard," "Visiting
Cold Mountain," "On Being Asked by a Blind Man Where the Restrooms
Are," "Testament"

Publisher: Leah Huete de Maines
Editor: Christen Kincaid
Cover Art and Design: Scott Finney
Author Photo: Scott Finney

Order online: www.finishinglinepress.com
also available on amazon.com

Author inquiries and mail orders:
Finishing Line Press
PO Box 1626
Georgetown, Kentucky 40324
USA

Table of Contents

At a Rest Stop on I-95 North

a Haitian family squeezes into a hatchback
stuffed with boxes and bags of clothes.
It rattles off, bald tires wobbling,
gray smoke billowing from a broken muffler.

If my father were sitting beside me,
he'd shake his head. Where was he going,
coming here from a farm in the old country,
only seventeen?

Five miles up the road I pass the hatchback
parked on the shoulder, hood up,
the family sitting on grass beside it.
No one will stop to help
except other Haitians. So they wait.

He lived in boarding houses with paisans;
never spoke of the well-to-do's scorn.
But I could feel it in his grip
crushing my hand when we arm-wrestled.

Thirty minutes later, a pick-up trying to pull
 a trailer twice its size loaded with furniture,
lumber, cinder blocks, and who knows what else
chugs in the right lane, slowing traffic.
The driver, a stocky man, is singing,
a Popeye forearm tapping the door.

On His Own Somewhere
My Brother, 1938-1942

My mother never thought of him as dead
but grown up, out on his own somewhere.
She imagines that where he lives an angel
of good fortune guides him. He's too young
to fight in Korea, too old for Nam
but just the right age to be on his high school
baseball team the year of the championship.
He takes life as it comes and is not tempted
by ambition. Like his father he is a barber.
He marries the first woman he dates and has
two children, both resembling his mother,
the older named after her. She pictures him
sitting on the floor beneath the Christmas tree
with his children as they open their gifts
or at a birthday party for his daughter,
guiding her hand as she cuts the cake.
He loves to bring his boy to the shop and watch
him play—in a customer chair pretending
to read the paper, jacking up a barber chair,
standing on the footrest and spinning around.
Blessed by the hand of fate, life's uncertainty
and chaos do not trouble him where he lives,
out on his own happy to be alive.

The Greatest Spaghetti Maker in the World

the foot-high black and silver trophy said,
presented to my mother after cooking
for the nurses at Sisters of Mercy Hospital
on Labor Day when I was eight.

Then there were the Sunday evening dinners
in our parish gym, its shiny floor scuffed
with tables and chairs, two hundred diners
able to glimpse Mom in the kitchen
as she moved from pot to pot, stirring
with her big wooden spoon, steam rising
above her and floating out to the gym;
the dinners so popular the Protestants came.

The parish priests stopped by unannounced;
Mom cooked them spaghetti, specially blessed
for the occasion. And to think I once believed
the priests chose me over all the other altar boys
to serve at marriages and solemn high masses
because of my Christ like recitation of prayers.

Tuesday and Friday were family spaghetti days,
the pasta spun around a fork on a spoon,
starting over if I didn't get it right
as if this task unlocked a charm
that brought good health and love.

The day my father died he shuffled to the kitchen
pulling his tank and sat at the table
so he could watch Mom lay spaghetti on his plate,
the sauce bubbling, the buttery aroma
        lingering in the steam.

Smart

My father wanted to be smart. Like Rockefeller.
He invested in oil wells that gushed for one day then died.
He owned a share of a copper mine that no one could find.
Then there was the strip mall built on land he sold too soon
and the furniture warehouse on a farm ten miles
from the nearest town. He never got smart.
He wanted his sons to be smart, be in business together.
"Three brothers should be like one," he'd say, raising
a hand with three fingers touching. We never got smart.
In his last days a nurse came to our house to help out.
I told her stories about his life as he sat in bed.
He'd rub his thumb across his fingers and smile.

Things You Left
—For my father

A photo of you wearing a miner's hat;
high cheek bones, thick brows, dark hair—
my inheritance staring at me.
Hidden beneath the hat, the six-point blue star
on your forehead from a knockout hit of coal
that put you out of work for a month.

A boxing glove, torn and faded,
autographed by Carmen Basilio,
a farmer as you once had been.
The night he fought Sugar Ray and went down
you sprang from your chair and yelled at the TV
No choice, no choice, you have to get back up.

A cathedral radio. You'd tap the webbed
heart-shaped speaker and say, *World War II
came out of there—boy soldiers dying,
the world falling apart.* Did you mean
just as your own boy was dying,
your heart falling apart?

A wooden cigar box filled with loose change
and old lottery tickets. It's where I kept
my baseball cards from the 1950s
before you threw them out.

A rosary with brown wooden beads
and a gold crucifix, touched with
fifty years of Hail Marys to guide my fate.
The same rosary that slipped from your pocket
as you filled gallon jugs at a spa.
You thought spring water was a cure.

I Remember Best

Ottavia Scutti, 1910-1993

I remember best the ways you cried—
torrents of tears to mourn a death,
a handkerchief pressed to your nose
waving off everyone who tried to console;
a tear trickling down your face drawn
with worry when I was sick, your hand
stroking my chest; or glassy-eyed
with mystery, waving goodbye.

On your first day in heaven I see you
in a garden at sunrise, picking Swiss chard
and eggplant to cook for my delight.
Midday you sit in your sewing room
beneath a skylight view, finishing by hand
a tablecloth embroidered with angels.

My Brother's Poetry

His kitchen floor is filled with tools—drills,
saws, hammers, wrenches; an angle grinder,
orbit sander, oxyacetylene welder.

He can replace brakes, carburetors,
clutches on cars, install air conditioners
and heaters, rebuild a motorcycle from scratch

with scavenged parts, hydraulic forks
to brakes, engine to exhaust pipe to wheels,
as if he were playing with toys.

Once I watched him install a water heater.
He walked around the tank, studying it
and then as he worked he tried futilely

to explain what he was doing. During a break
I asked how he learned to do all this.
He said it's easy. I look at the thing

like this heater and its parts—pipes, valves,
water tubes, thermostat, backstop, then I
picture the tools needed to match—pipe wrench,

tube cutter, solder torch, meter tester.
I told him I bend every nail I try to hammer.
He said I read too many books.

Whenever I visit I see a new tool, the last time
a drive click torque wrench. I asked what it was for.
He said he didn't know yet, that sometimes

"I see the match before I see the thing."

Home
Altino, Italy

1

My parents never returned to visit their hometown
before they died. Now I walk their streets
and alleys nodding and waving at townsmen
with thick brows and high cheekbones like mine;
the alleys dating to medieval time,
legend has it, a mix of cobblestones

and tuff cutting a narrow path through rows
of houses inches apart as if they were one.
I stop at the house where my mother was born,
the white plaster front in her pictures now beige
with red shutters and a matching tile roof,
embellishments her father would have scorned.

I recall his picture standing beside my parents
on their wedding day, his chest bulging from
his suit, bald with a pencil mustache, his eyes
a distant glare, worried perhaps his daughter
was being taken to a strange land by a dreamer.

2

The church of Santa Maria del Popolo
where my parents met overlooks the town
like a shepherd on a hill guarding his flock.
Inside, I climb to the choir loft and sit at the organ,
rest my hands on the keys. My godfather was once
the organist and played at my parent's wedding.

I look out to the sanctuary, the altar bordered
on each side by Corinthian columns
beneath Jesus in agony on a cross
that looks as large as the real one. The cross
was built by my grandfather from a tree
he cut down himself a century ago.

3

The town's highest point looks over a valley
of olive trees lining a dirt road, eastward
to the farm where my father was born and west
to the highway to Naples and a ship
to the new world. I imagine living here,
a carpenter, a farmer faithful to my hands,

no fear of failure burning in my lungs,
nowhere to hide. I'd know my place, here
among the humble. But would I stay? No.
I'd take the highway as my father had done
and return unsure of what I was looking for,
just a feeling stirring in my blood, his blood.

Family Planet

Having chosen a solitary life,
I've fallen off my family's planet.
All these nephews, nieces, their children,
cousins and their children laughing
and hugging at yet another wedding,
most unaware I'm the uncle of the bride.

They don't care to second-guess their fate
or try my life-prolonging regimen
of veggies and Zen: whatever they need
God will provide. With middle age
they'll let their bodies out and paint
their graying hair in elegant arrays.
They'll be patriarchs and matriarchs
in their final years, shrinking inward
only a breath away from heaven

where they will listen as their children
promise to remember them,
smile as their children forget them,
and wait for the planet to come to a stop
before it spins again, with or without me.

The Mystery Couple

He'd chase us out of his woods shouting
Goddamn punks. On the street, scowling,
he'd point at every boy he passed, each one
a trespasser, trampling plants, snooping.
She appeared on Fridays strolling
to the bank, wearing seamed black nylons
and a black dress, rouge caked in wrinkles,
lipstick smeared around a weak smile.

Inside a stone-walled house hidden
behind spruces and firs and enclosed
by a chain-link fence, their secrets were safe.
Only the woods threatened, smelling
of warm earth and mint with tree ferns
wrapped in arms of ivy, robins' eggs
in fallen nests, and now and then
a copperhead sliding into a shrub,
hiding, showing its head, hiding again.

Verotti Construction

In his prime Verotti could drive a nail
through a two-by-four with his hand;
a craft honed as steel pressed skin
to bone and layers of callous grew
year by year like rings in an oak
until pain and power breathed as one.

Now, wheezing with every breath,
his sons running the business,
he sits in his garden beneath clusters
of grapes growing on an arbor
where he can reach out and touch
his escarole, zucchini, and tomatoes
ripe on the vine, a heaven only God
could match and worth every nail.

Little Flower
Theresa Patrone, 1928-1970

I've been working since I was fifteen
when Daddy died, thirteen years now.
I clean the rectory on Friday, the church
on Saturday. Our pastor nods and smiles
when he sees me as if I were a saint.
At Mass on weekdays I hear him growl
at the altar boys. But everyone likes him.
He has slot machines in the church basement,
gambles and drinks wine with old ladies.

I like Father Haley best, the youngest.
He's outside when I clean the rectory,
tossing a tennis ball against a wall
then running half-heartedly to catch it
as if he didn't care. I think his heart
is troubled. Maybe he has a woman,
a secret lover he meets at night
in Memorial Park by the lake.

Mom pretends to be holy, sitting in her faded
mourning dress, too fat to kneel, head bowed,
lips faking prayers. While I clean she sits
and dozes, then takes all the money. She says
do little things with love and God will bless me,
like Little Flower, St. Therese, my patron saint.

I want to be like Rita Hayworth.
Her brown eyes and hair are just like mine.
In bed at night I see Stuart Granger press her
to his chest in Salome. Then I see the sexton,
Andrew, winking at me as I dust the choir loft.

I skip benches when I mop and never scrape
the wax from candleholders. When I pray
I see men smiling at me. At Mass I love
to stare at the stained-glass windows
depicting the stations of the cross
gleaming in the morning sun as I sit
beneath Veronica wiping the face of Jesus,
the light kissing my neck and shoulders.

At the Abbott's Frozen Custard Stand

The old people, wearing Bolo name tags,
sit in the shade facing the senior care bus
gleaming in the distance. Millie's face
appears to rest on her silver puff of hair
as she looks up at a spoon of chocolate
held by an aide, her mouth like a little girl's
accepting the host. Eyes closed beneath
a WW II cap, Luke slouches on his scooter,
his tongue circling a double mango with chips.
Kay dozes in her wheelchair, a smile peeping
beneath her bowed head and brunette wig.
His hand trembling, Dr. Norman Marks
scoops from a cup and raises an empty spoon,
each rep easier, building momentum.

Luke is first to go—bracing the handlebars,
head aimed at the bus, tipping his hat
when he reaches the lift door. Shuffling,
an aide holding an arm, Millie waves
to children and mothers on the walk up
squabbling over flavors and toppings.
Still asleep, smiling, Kay is whisked away.
Dr. Marks balances on his walker,
unsteady at first. He starts cautiously,
then steps faster and faster, the wheels
rolling smoothly, to the door's dark mouth.

Great Blue Heron

He waits, solitary, still,
knee deep in shallows.
He snags a minnow, displays it.
Wings flapping like the sound
of marching, his shadow sails
over water and onto land.
Gray sticks of legs slink
across my yard, stopping where I sit.

A black BB eye inspects me,
beak tilted up as if to say, So?
And then a goodbye, crackling
his four-beat diminuendo.

Now he perches on a mangrove's
highest limb and sweeps his beak
like the second hand of a clock
semi-circling, the limb holding firm
as if its burden is only a spirit.

Wood Stork

Always hungry, hunting in shallows,
lakes, even stagnant canals by highways,
a big guy, white with strokes of black
beneath his wings, a gnarled iron wedge
for a head, his beak a foot-long poniard,
ideal to strike and swallow in a flash,
his specialty. He can multi-task,
spraying waste while scratching his beak,
all on one leg. That thing must be itchy.
They say he's loyal to his mate
and helps in the nest, sitting on the eggs.
Sometimes I see them hunting together.
When I approach, she flies away.
He waits until I come within ten feet,
then chicken lopes a safe distance—
Groucho striding across a stage,
a long Havana dangling from his lips.

MIA

1951

I'd picture him in the cockpit cold and alone
lost in the night sky as we prayed
at children's mass for his safe return.
William was an altar boy, our pastor had said.
His brother was an usher; when he reached
across my pew with the offering basket
I'd turn away, escaping his eyes.

Sometimes after school I'd stop at their house
hidden behind pines and spruces,
just down the street from the church.
I'd walk to the steps, never seeing
or hearing anything alive, the silence
like our prayers waiting for God's hand
to open and guide William back to us.

Playing War
(Prospect Hill Churchyard)

I stand behind a gravestone
sniping, my broomstick rifle
popping like a tommy gun.
Rusty sounds like a shotgun—
a hammer pounding wood,
Rail like a hawk—*keeyah keeyah*.

Scooter sounds confused,
his rat-a-tat-tat breaking off
suddenly. Big Mike fires
in volleys of two and three,
smooth, well timed. We fire

one on one, we fire helter-
skelter, whistle, chug and groan:
bullets strafe dirt, pound trunks
of trees, carom off stones
near the hedgerows, the church,
the graves until dusk brings silence.

Night Shift, Big Steel

c. Summer 1964

Cranes on rails roar like El trains,
smoking strips of steel slide to a molder,
the moon peeks through windows.

My feet burn as I rake coal in the furnace.
Blount, the foreman can see me through air holes
in the door, ready to pounce if I slacken.

An hour in hell and then I shovel steel dust,
damp in piles, clogging my nose, soaking
my lungs, pinching like ants inside my jockeys.

I watch old Jeb twirl a hoisting chain
around a bundle of pipe with his crane hook
as graceful as Chaplin spinning his cane.

He likes to talk retirement. Pallid skin,
black teeth, a cigarette between his lips
I see him in a casket cuddling a crane hook.

Reverend Rufus, who always works at night
to be closer to God, sweeps toward me
in circles, dancing, the broom his partner.

He pushes me against a wall.
The low shall be high, trust the Lord, he says
reeking of whiskey, bloodshot eyes bulging.

Moonlight spills to the floor, edges toward me,
a rising tide marking the time—
four hours to go, and two more weeks.

The shop steward, Torko, an oak with legs
lumbers toward me, stops and says
Hope you're having fun college boy.

Perimeter Guard

They put me in the west tower,
a dark furnace. It smells like piss.
In the village all I see are campfires.
But I know where Charlie is—
hiding in the grass near the wire
taunting me, wailing and crowing,
piercing the night like the heat.
Sometimes a flare streaks the sky in red
breaking the boredom, and I'll sneak a smoke.

When my troop plane landed in Nam a guy yelled
"I don't believe this is happening to me,"
and everyone laughed. I feel like him.
He was headed for the Big Red One,
a grunt like me. I wonder if he's still alive.

On patrol last month Rusty stepped on a mine,
shattering his legs. He said "Ah shit" then died.
The day Monk took two bullets in his chest, he left
a smile, it seemed, dead on his back in the paddy.

In Nha Trang I watched the protestors on TV—
all those pretty girls. If I get back,
I'll have a ponytail and a Fu Manchu.
I'll sleep all day then cruise for chicks till dawn.

They say the CO has insomnia.
Maybe he's awake now, listening
to Charlie Parker on his stereo.

Route 19 West

Qui Nhon. By sunrise I'm soaked with sweat until night.
Beer cans in gutters clog the flow of urine.
Shrines—coke cans and grass in crates—are everywhere.
But no one ever prays.

Phu Cat. Papa-san squats in a rice paddy, smiles.
I snap a picture of black and yellow teeth.
A stench of dung and smoke sticks in the air.

Binh Dinh. Mama-san staggers across the road,
baskets of rice swaying beneath her shoulder bar.
The fragile bones and withered skin of her arms
have no voice to cry.

An Khe. An overturned jitney blocks the road,
wheels spinning, bodies squirming to get out.
My help is refused. They want candy, cigarettes.

Pleiku. The big guns of night ring in my ears,
shake my hootch. I smell fire. I dream of fire.

Foghorn

In the county where I grew up each town
had a volunteer fire company and a firehouse
with a foghorn alarm. In multiple alarms
the horns clashed in a din of drones, bellows,
grunts and bongs until our town's horn surpassed
the others, its sound like pounding piano keys.

My father told me stories of the town's great fires:
Saint Jude Church choking in flames as firemen
rushed inside to save the tabernacle and altarpiece;
the day the fire company lost Flip, the milkman
when the B&O warehouse toppled; the explosion
that destroyed Woolworths, bits of red glass
from its storefront found a hundred yards away.

Now while I sit in my car as a pumper
and aerial ladder speed past, cutting lanes,
red lights flashing, I can hear the foghorn
in counterpoint with the wailing sirens.

A Tavern in Shiraz

> *Those who change lead into gold with a mere wink of their eyes. Oh God, would that they glance at us from the corner of their eyes.*
> *—Hafez*

The insults of the rich are subtle, Hafez.
If they glance at me from the corner of their eyes,

they mean to say there's nothing I can do
to impress them - as if I were a shadow.

Their handshakes are firm, certain of everything,
and their prayers are always answered.

You say Midas suffered for his lust of gold.
These days gold can buy a life of piety.

My bitterness is not envy, as you surmise.
I don't want their riches, only my dignity.

You say the secret of salvation is forgiveness of flaws.
I can't forgive what I can't forget. Why lie?

But the wine is tasty today, Hafez,
to soothe our troubled hearts.

Visiting Cold Mountain
Chekiang Province, China

You were asleep, Han-Shan, resting your head
against a ginkgo when I first saw you.
I didn't know it was you until you said
Lay your alms by the hermit's cave.
If I had known, I would have left
a peck of rice and a jug of wine.

Lucky you lived twelve hundred years ago.
Now the earth itself is dying.
Where I live the river behind my home
has been poisoned with sewage and fertilizer.
Algae look like pea soup and smell like mold
and turtles have lumps on their heads.
Those responsible for this should be exiled
to a mountain top and forced to listen to rain.

I wish I could live as you did,
watching plum blossoms bloom
as you waited for wine's wisdom to guide you.
But time moves too fast.
Memory seems like a myth or nothing at all
and friends and their offers of kindness are mist.

On Being Asked by a Blind Man
Where the Restrooms Are

You have a guide dog, I say. He's confused,
misdirected, he says. I lead him
down the hallway, holding his arm.
I want to ask whether it's true that the blind
have no sense of time. But I say
nice dog, there's more to life than snacks
and play and a good belly scratch.

I tell him what I look like; he touches my cheek.
I wonder what he would give up to see.

Testament

I know how doctors use cold science
and cost analysis to pick the time to pull
the plugs. I designate someone ambivalent
who'd rather wait an extra day or two.

Cremation scares me. Pounds of powder
in a shoeshine box or tossed to the wind.
I hate the wind, slapping greenery,
gusting and howling, mixing the scent
of evergreens with the stench of rot.
I like to think of the day, the sun baking
the ground, when I saw a pine tree
behind an old grave, giving shade.

Ground burial is fine, but please don't leave
roses or lilies. They remind me of funerals.
I'd like a gravestone. Nothing fancy,
just enough for birds to perch.
Once I saw a Bachman's sparrow
singing on a faded stone, his whistle
changing pitch trill to trill. Bring seed.

Jim Scutti's poetry and fiction has appeared in numerous literary magazines, including *Comstock Review, The Main Street Rag, FutureCycle Poetry, Common Ground Review, The Rattling Wall* and *Slant*. He practiced law prior to retiring and now devotes most of his time to writing, reading and running. He lives on the Indian River in Vero Beach, Florida.

www.ingramcontent.com/pod-product-compliance
Lightning Source LLC
Chambersburg PA
CBHW022059080426
42734CB00009B/1410